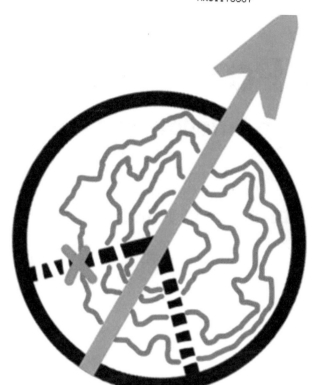

A Path-Maker

An Unfollowable Path

Dr. Aaron C. Waldron, M.Div.

A Path-Maker

An Unfollowable Path

Dr. Aaron C. Waldron, M.Div.

Lost Raven Studios

Title: A Path-Maker: An Unfollowable Path

Author: Dr. Aaron C. Waldron, M.Div.

Publication Date: 2024

Available Formats: Ebook (PDF & ePub,) and Paperback

ISBN: 978-1-964313-02-3 (Paperback Book)

About Lost Raven Studios: Lost Raven Studios is dedicated to publishing works that explore the intersection of spirituality, psychology, and personal growth. Our mission is to provide readers with transformative insights and practical guidance for navigating life's complexities and discovering deeper meaning. Through innovative storytelling and deep spiritual wisdom, Lost Raven Studios invites readers to embark on journeys of Self-discovery and healing.

Contact Information:

Website: Lost Raven Studios.com

Email: LostRavenStudios@Gmail.com

Dedicated to

Those who feel like outcast, different,

strange or just never fit in.

To my life partner, thank you for

showing me the part of me we couldnt see.

To anyone traversing life off-path.

Contents

Chapter 1

The Path-Maker Symbol

The Path-Maker symbol is a powerful emblem representing a Path-Makers journey of life and the process of becoming. At its foundation is a **black closed circle**, *symbolizing the circle of life, signifying completeness, cycles, and the continuous journey we all undertake. Overlaying the circle is a* **blue compass arrow,** *pointing to "true north," which represents a guiding principle, direction, or goal, symbolizing moral or ethical direction, a purposeful path, or a Spirit Led Methodology. Within this circle are* **red contour lines,** *illustrating both the mapped and unmapped terrain that Path-Makers navigate. These lines signify the known challenges and achievements (mapped terrain) as well as the unknown opportunities and obstacles (unmapped terrain) encountered along the journey. Intersecting the circle and the compass arrow are* **two black dashed lines forming a 90-degree**

angle. *These lines represent the planned and current paths, symbolizing intentions, goals, and strategies (planned path) alongside the ongoing journey and reality of progress (current path). At the heart of this Theopoetic symbol lies a* **brown "X" mark**, symbolizing a multi-dimensional destination—a theopoetic pursuit of a place that never truly exists yet feels profoundly real. This "X" *symbolizes the eternal quest for meaning and fulfillment, a journey toward an ever-elusive destination that beckons us forward. Together, these elements create* **a Theopoetic symbol**, a meta-spiritual symbol that embodies the completeness of life, the pursuit of true direction, the exploration of both known and unknown challenges, and the sacred interplay between Spirit and purpose.

A Path-Maker

Becoming a **Path-Maker** is a **Multi-Faith Journey towards Self.** It implies embracing a transformative and inclusive approach to spirituality and personal growth. A Path-Maker is someone who Theopoetically navigates the complicated landscapes of various faith traditions, seeking wisdom, understanding, and Self-discovery along the way. Here are key aspects that define the essence of a Path-Maker:

Open-minded Exploration: A Path-Maker is open to exploring the rich tapestry of diverse spiritual traditions without prejudice. They value the unique insights each faith offers and recognize the potential for personal growth

through exposure to different perspectives.

Seeking Truth & Common Ground: Instead of focusing solely on differences, a Path-Maker actively seeks commonalities and universal truths shared among different faiths. They recognize the underlying principles that unite humanity, fostering a sense of interconnectedness.

Personal Growth & Transformation: The Multi-Faith journey is not just about intellectual exploration but also about personal transformation. A Path-Maker uses the teachings and practices from various traditions as tools for self-discovery, personal development, and spiritual growth.

Respectful Dialogue: Engaging in respectful and empathetic dialogue is a hallmark of a Path-Maker. They appreciate the diversity of beliefs and engage in conversations that promote understanding, building bridges rather than walls.

Integration of Wisdom: A Path-Maker integrates the wisdom gained from different faiths into their daily life. This integration is not about syncretism but rather a mindful incorporation of values and practices that resonate with their own journey towards self-realization.

Compassionate Engagement: Compassion is a guiding principle for a Path-Maker. They understand that each individual's spiritual journey is unique, and they approach others with empathy, creating a supportive community where everyone can flourish.

Embracing Uncertainty: The multi-faith journey often involves navigating ambiguity and uncertainty. A Path-Maker is comfortable with the unknown, understanding that the journey towards Self is a continual process of discovery and growth.

Being a Path-Maker is about transcending boundaries, fostering unity, and recognizing the inherent interconnectedness of all spiritual paths on the journey towards a deeper understanding of Self and the World.

The Path-Maker archetype possesses a deep understanding of the meta-spiritual/multi-faith aspects of existence. They recognize that spirituality extends beyond organized religion and dogma, embracing diverse philosophies and practices. They embody the exploration of the interconnectedness of all beings, the importance of intuitive wisdom, and the recognition of one's unique path. They guide others to transcend conventional beliefs, encouraging exploration and open-mindedness. The Path-Maker archetype represents an individual regardless of gender, sexuality, race or class who dives into the waters of meta-spirituality, surpassing the colonized boundaries of organized religion and dogma. They possess a profound understanding of the spiritual aspects of existence, acknowledging that spirituality encompasses a broader spectrum of philosophies and practices. At the core of their belief system lies the recognition of the interconnectedness of all beings. They perceive the underlying unity that binds humanity, nature, and the cosmos together. This perspective enables them to see beyond superficial differences and embrace the inherent oneness that permeates all existence. The Path-Maker embodies this interconnectedness in their thoughts, actions, and interactions, fostering a sense of harmony and compassion in their relationships with others.

One of the key qualities of the Path-Maker archetype is their emphasis on **intuitive wisdom**. They recognize that there is a deep well of knowledge and guidance within each individual, accessible through intuition and inner knowing. They encourage others to tap into this inner wisdom, helping them trust their instincts and develop a strong sense of Self-trust. The Path-Maker understands that intuitive insights can lead to profound personal growth, spiritual awakening, and a greater alignment with one's authentic path. Furthermore, the Path-Maker archetype recognizes and respects the unique journey of everyone. They understand that each person has their own path to follow, shaped by their experiences, desires, and innate gifts. Rather than imposing rigid beliefs or predefined paths, the Path-Maker guides others to explore and discover their own truth. They encourage open-mindedness, fostering an environment where individuals can freely question, explore, and synthesize various spiritual perspectives.

In their role as guides, the Path-Maker archetype assists others in transcending conventional beliefs and limitations. They encourage individuals to expand their horizons, challenge preconceived notions, and step outside their comfort zones. This process of exploration and expansion opens new possibilities for personal and spiritual growth. **The Path–Maker helps individuals navigate the complexities of their spiritual journey, providing support, wisdom, and encouragement along the way.** Overall, the Path-Maker archetype represents a deep and multifaceted understanding of spirituality that extends beyond religious institutions and dogmatic practices. They embody the interconnectedness of all beings, emphasize intuitive wisdom, honor individual paths, and inspire others to transcend conventional beliefs. By embracing a meta-spiritual perspective, the Path-Maker archetype guides individuals towards a more expansive and authentic spiritual experience, fostering personal growth, and cultivating a greater sense of connection and purpose.

Strengths

Individuality & Authenticity: The Path-Maker archetype champions individuality, emphasizing the importance of embracing one's true Self and unique gifts. They inspire others to break free from societal expectations, allowing for authentic Self-expression and personal growth.

Transformational Catalysts: They serve as catalysts for personal and collective transformation, encouraging others to challenge their limiting beliefs, expand their consciousness, and evolve spiritually. Their guidance and wisdom inspire profound shifts in perspectives and behaviors, igniting inner change and awakening.

Intuitive Guidance: The Path-Maker archetype possesses heightened intuition, offering intuitive insights and guidance to those they mentor. They have a deep connection with their inner wisdom and the spiritual realm, helping individuals navigate their own inner journeys with clarity and compassion.

Bridge Builders: They bridge the gap between the spiritual and physical worlds, effectively communicating spiritual concepts and experiences in relatable ways. They translate complex ideas into practical wisdom, making spirituality accessible and relevant to people's daily lives.

Weaknesses

Isolation and Misunderstanding: The Path-Maker archetype may feel isolated or misunderstood due to their unique perspectives and unconventional beliefs. They may struggle to find like-minded individuals or face resistance from those who fear change or challenge traditional norms.

Personal Burdens: The responsibility of guiding and inspiring others can be emotionally and energetically demanding. The Path-Maker archetype may sometimes neglect their own Self-care, prioritizing the well-being of others over their own needs.

Impatience: Their deep desire for transformation and growth may lead to impatience with others who are not yet ready or receptive to change. They must learn to honor each person's unique journey and respect the pace of individual transformation.

Significance

The Path-Maker archetype plays a significant role in advocating for individuality and inspiring transformation within their communities. They challenge the status quo, encouraging others to question societal norms and embrace their true selves. By fostering an environment of growth and Self-realization, they empower individuals to explore their own spiritual paths, discover their unique gifts, and express their authentic nature. The Path-Maker archetype also embarks on their own inward journey, continuously seeking personal growth and Self-transformation. Their own quest for truth and Self-realization serves as an inspiration to others, demonstrating the transformative power of embracing one's individual path. Through their strengths and weaknesses, the Path-Maker archetype creates a ripple effect of change, helping individuals and communities evolve spiritually, embrace their uniqueness, and create a more harmonious and awakened world.

The Path-Makers Departure from the Conventional

The Path-Maker's journey commences with a departure from the conventional, the known, and the established norms. By deviating from the well-worn path, they embrace uncertainty, fully aware that they are about to embark on a unique and uncharted exploration. **This act of stepping away from the expected and normalized signifies their commitment to personal growth and the pursuit of a higher truth.** It is through this departure that the Path-Maker sets the stage for the transformative leadership they will come to embody. The departure of the Path-Maker from the conventional signifies a bold and courageous step towards personal growth and Self-discovery. They recognize that clinging to the familiar and conforming to established norms can limit their potential and confine them within the boundaries of mediocrity. By venturing into uncharted territory, the Path-Maker embraces uncertainty and willingly exposes themselves to the unknown. This act of departure demonstrates their willingness to take risks and their commitment to breaking free from the confines of the ordinary.

Stepping away from the expected and normalized also indicates the Path-Maker's rejection of societal pressures and external influences that may hinder their individuality and authentic expression. They understand that true fulfillment and meaningful progress often lie beyond the confines of conventional thinking. By breaking away from the well-trotted path, the Path-Maker declares their intention to forge their own unique journey, one that aligns with their inner values, aspirations, and vision. The departure from the conventional not only serves as an act of rebellion against conformity but also as a catalyst for personal transformation. It challenges the Path-Maker to question deeply ingrained beliefs, ideologies, and assumptions that may have shaped their worldview. This departure encourages critical thinking and the exploration of alternative perspectives, opening up new avenues of understanding and knowledge. The departure sets the stage for the Path-Maker's transformative leadership. By willingly embracing uncertainty and venturing into the unknown, they develop resilience, adaptability, and the capacity to navigate uncharted territories. Their willingness to challenge the status quo inspires others to question and reevaluate their own paths, fostering a culture of innovation and growth.

Moreover, the departure from the conventional allows the Path-Maker to uncover hidden potentials within themselves. They tap into their creativity and intuition, exploring new possibilities and pushing the boundaries of what is considered possible. This exploration not only benefits the Path-Maker but also enables them to bring unique insights, ideas, and solutions to the communities and organizations they lead. By departing from the conventional, the Path-Maker embarks on a profound journey of Self-discovery, growth, and leadership. They embody the spirit of exploration, embracing uncertainty and embracing the transformative power of charting their own course. Through their departure, the Path-Maker becomes a beacon of inspiration, inviting others to embrace their individuality, challenge norms, and pave their own paths towards personal and collective greatness.

The Creation of an Unfollowable Path

As the Path-Maker traverses' unfamiliar terrain, they begin to carve out their own path— a path that is unfollowable. This path is not intended for others to replicate but serves as an invitation for individuals to discover and cultivate their own authentic journeys. The Path-Maker's trail is a symbol of inspiration, urging others to question societal norms, challenge their own limitations, and forge their unique paths and identity. They become living testimonies to the possibility of creating a life aligned with one's inner truth: God.

The creation of an unfollowable path by the Path-Maker goes beyond simply exploring unfamiliar terrain. It is a Sacred and deliberate act of carving out a unique path that cannot be replicated by others. The Path-Maker understands that each individual possesses their own set of experiences, talents, and aspirations, and as such, their journey cannot be duplicated. Instead, their path serves as an invitation for others to embark on their own authentic journeys. The Path-Maker's trail becomes a symbol of inspiration, a beacon that encourages individuals to question the established societal norms and colonized expectations that often dictate the choices and directions in life. By challenging these norms, individuals can break free from the constraints placed upon them and discover their true potential. The Path-Maker's path is a testament to the limitless possibilities that lie outside the boundaries of conformity.

In carving their own unfollowable path, the Path-Maker also encourages others to confront and transcend their own limitations. They serve as living examples that one's potential is not determined by external factors or preconceived notions but is rather a reflection of their own determination, resilience, and willingness to explore uncharted territories. The Path-Maker's journey inspires others to embrace the discomfort of uncertainty and to embrace personal growth and Self-discovery. The unfollowable path is not solely about physical journeys or external accomplishments. It extends deeper into the realm of personal identity and Self-realization. The Path-Maker's trail invites individuals to forge their unique paths, not only in terms of external achievements but also in terms of understanding and aligning with their inner truth. It recognizes that true fulfillment comes from living a life that resonates with one's deepest values, passions, and purpose.

The unfollowable path also evokes a spiritual dimension. By aligning their journey with their inner truth, the Path-Maker acknowledges a higher power or divine presence. They recognize that the pursuit of an authentic life is not separate from the concept of God or a higher purpose. Instead, it becomes a harmonious integration of personal growth, Self-expression, and connection to something greater than oneself. In essence, the creation of an unfollowable path by the Path-Maker is a transformative process that transcends conventional notions of success and achievement. It is an invitation for individuals to embark on their own unique journeys, challenging societal norms, embracing personal growth, and aligning with their inner truth and the divine. By embracing the unfollowable path, individuals can become architects of their own lives, crafting an existence that is deeply fulfilling, purposeful, and in harmony with their authentic selves and the higher forces that guide them.

Decentralized Leadership in Community

Unlike traditional leaders who command from a centralized position, the Path-Maker's leadership style is decentralized. They do not seek followers or adherents but instead empower others to become the architects of their own destinies. **The Path-Maker's presence in the community acts as a catalyst for change, nurturing a collective spirit of Self-discovery and Self-empowerment.** Through their example, they challenge the notion of hierarchical leadership, fostering an environment that encourages every individual to embrace their innate potential and contribute to the growth of the whole.

Decentralized leadership in the context of community, as exemplified by the Path-Maker, represents a departure from the traditional top-down approach to leadership. Rather than commanding and directing others, the Path-Maker adopts a more inclusive and empowering style of leadership. This decentralized leadership style is characterized by several key aspects that foster a sense of community and enable individuals to take ownership of their own growth and development. Firstly, the Path-Maker does not seek followers or adherents in the traditional sense. They do not strive to create a hierarchy where they hold all the power and authority. Instead, they act as a catalyst for change by inspiring and empowering others. Their role is to facilitate and support the growth of individuals within the community, encouraging them to become architects of their own destinies. This approach creates a sense of ownership and personal investment among community members, as they actively participate in shaping their own lives and the collective future.

The presence of the Path-Maker in the community serves as a source of inspiration and guidance. **They lead by example, demonstrating the values and principles they espouse.** Through their actions and behaviors, they show others what is possible and challenge the conventional notions of hierarchical leadership. By rejecting the idea of a single central authority, the Path-Maker encourages individuals to tap into their own potential and contribute to the growth and well-being of the whole community. In a decentralized leadership model, every individual's unique skills, perspectives, and contributions are valued and encouraged. The Path-Maker fosters an environment that nurtures a collective spirit of Self-discovery and Self-empowerment. They create spaces for dialogue, collaboration, and open exchange of ideas, ensuring that everyone's voice is heard and respected. This inclusive approach allows for the emergence of diverse perspectives, creativity, and innovation within the community. By promoting decentralized leadership, the Path-Maker empowers individuals to embrace their innate potential. They encourage personal growth and provide opportunities for learning and development. Through mentorship, coaching, and guidance, they help community members discover their strengths, passions, and purpose. This individual growth, in turn, contributes to the overall growth and vitality of the community, as each person brings their unique talents and contributions to the collective table.

In summary, decentralized leadership in community, as embodied by the Path-Maker, represents a paradigm shift from traditional hierarchical leadership models. It emphasizes empowerment, inclusivity, and the cultivation of individual potential. By rejecting centralized authority and fostering a spirit of Self-discovery and Self-empowerment, the Path-Maker encourages every individual to take ownership of their own growth and contribute to the collective well-being. Through their decentralized leadership style, the Path-Maker creates a thriving community where everyone's voice is valued and where individuals are inspired to become architects of their own destinies.

Authenticity & the Power of Vulnerability

A core aspect of the Path-Maker's leadership lies in their unwavering authenticity. By embracing vulnerability, they inspire others to do the same, creating a space for genuine connection and growth. The Path-Maker's willingness to share their own trials and tribulations allows community members to recognize their shared humanity and overcome societal pressures to conform. In doing so, the Path-Maker dismantles the illusion of separateness and establishes an atmosphere of trust, fostering collective growth and transformation. Authenticity and the power of vulnerability are profound qualities that play a vital role in the leadership style of the Path-Maker. These qualities go beyond surface-level interactions and have the potential to create deep, meaningful connections within a community or organization. At the heart of the Path-Maker's authenticity is a genuine and unwavering commitment to being true to oneself. They embrace their own imperfections and vulnerabilities, recognizing that these aspects of their humanity do not diminish their worth or ability to lead. Instead, they view vulnerability as a strength, understanding that it allows them to connect on a deeper level with others. By openly sharing their own trials and tribulations, the Path-Maker creates a safe space for others to do the same. This vulnerability not only encourages others to be authentic but also helps them recognize that their struggles and challenges are not isolated experiences. In this way, the Path-Maker cultivates a sense of shared humanity within the community.

Society often imposes pressures to conform, encouraging individuals to present a polished and flawless facade. However, the Path-Maker's willingness to be vulnerable challenges this societal norm. Their authenticity disrupts the illusion of separateness and perfection, offering an alternative narrative that embraces the messy and imperfect aspects of life. In this atmosphere of trust and authenticity, community members feel empowered to express their true selves without fear of judgment or rejection. This fosters a culture of acceptance and openness, where people can explore their potential, take risks, and grow. **The Path-Maker's vulnerability acts as a catalyst for personal and collective transformation, inspiring others to step out of their comfort zones and embrace**

their own authentic journeys. Furthermore, the Path-Maker's leadership style encourages a shift from a hierarchical power dynamic to a more inclusive and collaborative approach. Their vulnerability humanizes them and removes the barriers that typically separate leaders from their followers. This creates a sense of equality and shared responsibility within the community, empowering individuals to actively participate in the growth and development of the collective.

Ultimately, the power of vulnerability lies in its ability to forge deep connections, foster trust, and dismantle colonized expectations. Through their authenticity, the Path-Maker cultivates an environment where individuals can embrace their true selves and contribute to the collective journey of growth and transformation. By embracing vulnerability as a strength, the Path-Maker inspires others to do the same, unlocking their full potential and creating a more authentic and compassionate community or organization.

Chapter 2

How to Be a Path-Maker

Embark on a Multi-Faith journey of Self-exploration and Self-discovery. Reflect on your own beliefs, values, and experiences. Seek to understand your strengths, passions, and purpose. Explore the aspects of your identity that have been influenced by external systems and ideologies and discern what aligns with your authentic Self. Self-exploration is a deeply personal and transformative process that involves diving into the core aspects of one's being to gain a deeper understanding of oneself. **It is an introspective journey that invites individuals to reflect on their beliefs, values, and experiences, ultimately leading to Self-discovery and personal growth.**

To embark on a journey of Self-exploration, it is essential to create space for introspection and reflection. This can be done through various practices such as journaling, meditation, or engaging in meaningful dialogue with trusted individuals. These practices allow for the exploration of thoughts, emotions, and memories, providing insights into one's inner world. During Self-exploration, it is important to examine one's beliefs and values. Beliefs are the thoughts and ideas that shape our perspectives and guide our actions, while values are the principles and qualities, we hold dear. By examining these belief systems and values, individuals can identify which ones are truly aligned with their authentic Self and which may have been influenced by external factors such as societal expectations, cultural norms, or family upbringing.

Moreover, Self-exploration involves uncovering one's strengths, passions, and purpose. Strengths are the innate abilities and talents that come naturally to us, while passions are the activities or subjects that ignite our enthusiasm and drive. Identifying these strengths and passions can help individuals discover what brings them joy and fulfillment. Additionally, exploring one's purpose involves understanding the deeper meaning and direction in life, the reason for one's existence, and the impact one wishes to make in the world. Self-exploration also entails examining the aspects of one's identity that have been shaped by external systems and ideologies. Society, culture, and various forms of colonization often influence our identities and shape our perceptions of ourselves. By critically evaluating these influences, individuals can discern which aspects truly resonate with their authentic Self and make conscious choices about how they want to define their identity. The process of Self-exploration is ongoing and evolving. It requires patience, curiosity, and Self-compassion. As individuals continue to explore and discover more about themselves, they may encounter moments of discomfort or challenge. However, these moments often serve as opportunities for growth and transformation.

In summary, Self-exploration is a profound journey that involves reflecting on beliefs, values, experiences, strengths, passions, and purpose. It requires individuals to examine the influences that shape their identity and discern what aligns with their authentic Self. By engaging in this process, individuals can cultivate a deeper understanding of themselves, leading to personal growth, authenticity, and a more fulfilling life.

Cultivate Vision & Courage

Develop a clear vision of the path you want to tread and the transformations you seek. Be courageous in challenging the status quo and taking risks to bring about change. Embody resilience, perseverance, and determination in the face of obstacles. Cultivating vision and courage is essential for personal and professional growth. It involves developing a clear understanding of your goals and aspirations and having the courage to pursue them despite the challenges and risks involved. Let's dive deeper into each aspect:

Vision:

Having a vision means having a clear sense of direction and purpose in life. It requires introspection and Self-reflection to identify what truly matters to you and what you want to achieve. A well-defined vision serves as a guiding light, providing clarity on the path you want to tread and the transformations you seek. To cultivate vision, you can engage in activities such as goal setting, creating a vision board, jour-

naling, meditating, or seeking inspiration from others who have achieved similar goals. Regularly revisiting and refining your vision ensures that you stay focused and motivated along your journey.

Courage:

Courage is the ability to confront fear, take risks, and challenge the status quo. It involves stepping outside of your comfort zone and embracing uncertainty. Cultivating courage requires a mindset shift, where you view challenges as opportunities for growth rather than obstacles to avoid. Building courage involves developing Self-belief, resilience, and a willingness to learn from failures. It means being open to new experiences, ideas, and perspectives. Surrounding yourself with supportive and like-minded individuals can also bolster your courage, as you can draw strength from their encouragement and shared experiences.

Challenging the Status Quo:

Bringing about change often requires questioning and challenging the status quo. It means not accepting things as they are, but instead seeking innovative solutions and pushing boundaries. This mindset enables you to identify opportunities for improvement and create positive transformations. Challenging the status quo may involve questioning traditional norms, seeking alternative perspectives, and advocating for change in your personal or professional environment. It requires the ability to think critically, problem-solve, and communicate effectively to convey your vision and gain support from others.

Taking Risks:

Courageous individuals are willing to take calculated risks to achieve their vision. They understand that growth and progress often come with a degree of uncertainty and potential failure. Taking risks involves stepping into the unknown, embracing ambiguity, and being open to learning from both successes and setbacks. While it's important to assess risks and make informed decisions, being overly cautious can hinder personal growth and limit your potential. By embracing calculated risks, you expand your comfort zone, acquire new skills, and gain valuable experiences that contribute to your development.

Resilience and Perseverance:

The path to achieving your vision is rarely smooth, and setbacks and obstacles are inevitable. Building resilience and perseverance is crucial to overcome these challenges and continue moving forward. Resilience enables you to bounce back from failures, adapt to change, and maintain a positive mindset despite setbacks. Perseverance involves staying committed to your vision and goals, even when faced with difficulties. It requires determination, discipline, and the ability to stay motivated in the face of adversity. Seeking support from mentors, practicing Self-care, and cultivating a growth mindset can all contribute to building resilience and perseverance.

In summary, cultivating vision and courage involves developing a clear vision, having the courage to challenge the status quo and take risks, and embodying resilience and perseverance. By embracing these qualities, you can navigate through obstacles, bring about positive change, and achieve personal and professional success.

Seek Knowledge & Wisdom

Engage in lifelong learning and seek wisdom from various sources. Study religious and spiritual traditions, philosophy, psychology, and other disciplines that can deepen your understanding of the human condition and the possibilities for growth and transformation. Seeking knowledge and wisdom is an inherent human desire to understand the world around us and to uncover deeper truths about existence. It involves engaging in a lifelong learning process and actively seeking wisdom from diverse sources. This pursuit goes beyond mere accumulation of information; it encompasses a holistic exploration of various disciplines and perspectives that can contribute to a deeper understanding of the human condition and our potential for personal growth and transformation.

To embark on this journey, one can start by studying religious and spiritual traditions. These traditions offer valuable insights into the nature of existence, ethics, morality, and the purpose of life. They provide frameworks for understanding the interconnectedness of individuals, communities, and the larger cosmos. Exploring different religious and spiritual teachings can help broaden one's perspective and foster a sense of empathy and compassion towards others. Additionally, philosophy plays a crucial role in the pursuit of knowledge and wisdom. Philosophical inquiry delves into fundamental questions about reality, consciousness, morality, and the nature of knowledge itself. By engaging with different philosophical schools of thought, one can develop critical thinking skills, learn to question assumptions, and cultivate a deeper understanding of the complexities of human existence.

Psychology is another discipline that can greatly contribute to the quest for wisdom. It investigates the workings of the human mind, emotions, behavior, and relationships. By studying psychology, individuals can gain insights into their own thought patterns, motivations, and biases, as well as develop a greater understanding of others. Psychological knowledge can aid in personal growth, enhancing Self-awareness, emotional intelligence, and interpersonal skills. Furthermore, the pursuit of wisdom extends beyond traditional disciplines. It involves exploring a wide range of knowledge sources, including literature, art, science, and history. These disciplines provide unique perspectives on the human experience, sparking curiosity, and nurturing creativity. Literature and art, for instance, can illuminate different facets of the human condition, offering profound insights into emotions, relationships, and societal issues. Science and history, on the other hand, provide empirical evidence and context for understanding the physical world and the patterns of human behavior throughout time.

Engaging in lifelong learning is essential to the ongoing quest for knowledge and wisdom. It requires an open and curious mindset, a willingness to challenge existing beliefs, and a dedication to continuous personal growth. Lifelong learning can take various forms, such as reading books, attending lectures, participating in discussions, taking courses, or seeking mentorship. It is a dynamic process that encourages intellectual and spiritual development, empowering individuals to navigate the complexities of life with greater clarity and wisdom.

In conclusion, seeking knowledge and wisdom involves an ongoing commitment to lifelong learning and a multidisciplinary exploration of various sources of wisdom. By studying religious and spiritual traditions, philosophy, psychology, and other disciplines, individuals can deepen their understanding of the human condition and unlock new possibilities for personal growth and transformation. Embracing this journey allows individuals to cultivate wisdom, broaden their perspectives, and make meaningful contributions to themselves and the world around them.

Foster Empathy & Compassion

Cultivate empathy and compassion for others on their own paths. Listen attentively to their stories, validate their experiences, and offer support and guidance when needed. Embrace the role of a compassionate listener and mentor. Fostering empathy and compassion involves more than just superficially acknowledging others' experiences and offering support. It requires a deep understanding and genuine connection with individuals, allowing you to truly comprehend their emotions, perspectives, and struggles. To elaborate on this concept, let's explore some key aspects and practices for cultivating empathy and compassion.

Active Listening: Being an empathetic and compassionate person starts with being an active listener. It involves fully engaging with the speaker, paying attention to their

words, tone, and non-verbal cues. By actively listening, you create a safe space for others to express themselves and feel heard. Practice withholding judgment and refrain from interrupting, allowing them to share their thoughts and emotions freely.

Validate Experiences: Validation plays a crucial role in empathy. It means acknowledging and accepting someone's experiences and feelings as valid and important, regardless of whether you personally relate to them. Validating others' experiences helps them feel understood and valued. You can offer validation by expressing empathy, using phrases like, "We understand how you feel" or "That sounds really challenging. It's okay to feel that way."

Cultivate Perspective-Taking: Developing empathy involves stepping outside of your own frame of reference and attempting to understand someone else's perspective. Perspective-taking allows you to see the world through their eyes, considering their unique background, beliefs, and experiences. This practice helps you grasp the reasons behind their emotions and actions, fostering a deeper sense of empathy.

Practice Emotional Intelligence: Emotional intelligence is the ability to recognize, understand, and manage both your own emotions and the emotions of others. By cultivating emotional intelligence, you become better equipped to empathize with others. Pay attention to subtle emotional cues and try to interpret them accurately. This awareness will enable you to respond in a compassionate and supportive manner.

Offer Support & Guidance: Compassion goes beyond just understanding others; it also involves offering support and guidance when needed. As a compassionate listener and mentor, you can provide a sense of comfort and reassurance to others. Be available to lend a helping hand, offer advice, or connect them with resources that may be beneficial. Show genuine care and willingness to assist them on their paths.

Practice Self-Reflection: To deepen your capacity for empathy and compassion, it's important to engage in regular Self-reflection. Take the time to examine your own biases, judgments, and assumptions. Reflect on your interactions with others and consider how you could have responded with greater empathy or compassion. By continuously working on your Self, you create an environment that fosters understanding and growth.

Extend Empathy to Different Perspectives: Empathy and compassion can be further enhanced by seeking out diverse perspectives and experiences. Actively engage with individuals from different backgrounds, cultures, and beliefs. This exposure broadens your understanding of the human experience and helps you challenge any preconceived notions or biases you may hold.

In summary, fostering empathy and compassion requires active listening, validating others' experiences, cultivating perspective-taking, practicing emotional intelligence, offering support and guidance, engaging in Self-reflection, and embracing diverse perspectives. **By integrating these practices into your interactions with others, you can truly become a compassionate listener, mentor, and advocate for understanding and kindness.**

Create Supportive Spaces

Establish safe and inclusive spaces where individuals can explore their own paths of transformation and liberation. Encourage open dialogue, active listening, and the sharing of diverse perspectives. Foster a sense of community and mutual support. Like **Public Space** [1]Creating supportive spaces is essential for promoting personal growth, transformation, and liberation. Such spaces should be safe and inclusive, allowing individuals to explore their own unique journeys and experiences. To elaborate on this concept, let's dive deeper into the key elements involved: establishing safe and inclusive spaces, encouraging open dialogue, active listening, and sharing diverse perspectives, and fostering a sense of community and mutual support. Creating a safe and inclusive space involves ensuring that everyone feels welcome, respected, and valued. This can be achieved by:

Setting Boundaries: Establishing clear guidelines that promote respectful and constructive communication is crucial. Boundaries might include principles such as active listening, avoiding personal attacks, and acknowledging and validating diverse experiences and perspectives.

1   Aaron Waldron, "Public Space," Mailchi.mp, 2024, https://mailchi.mp/719fccce969d/public-space.

Cultivating Trust: Building trust among participants is vital to create an environment where people feel comfortable sharing their thoughts and emotions. This can be done by modeling vulnerability, empathy, and non-judgmental behavior.

Addressing Power Dynamics: Recognizing and addressing power imbalances within the space is essential for inclusivity. This can involve actively amplifying marginalized voices, promoting equal participation, and ensuring decision-making processes are fair and transparent.

Encouraging Open Dialogue: Open dialogue allows individuals to engage in honest and meaningful conversations, fostering personal growth and understanding. Some key aspects of encouraging open dialogue include:

Active Participation: Encourage individuals to actively participate in discussions by sharing their thoughts, feelings, and experiences. Creating a non-hierarchical environment promotes equal opportunity for all participants to contribute.

Respectful Communication: Foster an atmosphere where respectful communication is valued. Encourage individuals to express their viewpoints while actively listening to others without interruption or judgment. Emphasize the importance of using "I" or "My" statements to express personal perspectives rather than generalizing.

Constructive Feedback: Promote the practice of giving and receiving constructive feedback. Encourage individuals to provide feedback that is specific, focused on behaviors or ideas, and aimed at promoting growth and understanding.

Sharing Diverse Perspectives: Creating spaces where diverse perspectives are shared and valued is essential for promoting empathy, understanding, and personal growth. Some strategies to facilitate this include:

Celebrating Differences: Encourage individuals to embrace and appreciate the diverse backgrounds, experiences, and identities of others. Recognize the value that different perspectives bring to the space.

Intersectionality: Promote an understanding of intersectionality, which acknowledges the interconnectedness of different social identities (e.g., race, gender, class, sexuality, ability). Encourage individuals to reflect on how their own experiences and privileges intersect with others, fostering a deeper appreciation for the complexity of lived experiences.

Experiential Learning: Provide opportunities for individuals to engage in experiential learning activities, such as storytelling, role-playing, or empathy exercises. These activities can help participants gain insights into different perspectives and cultivate empathy.

Fostering a Sense of Community & Mutual Support: Building a sense of community and mutual support is essential for individuals to feel connected, validated, and empowered. Some approaches to foster this sense of community include:

Building Relationships: Encourage individuals to build connections with one another through activities such as icebreakers, group projects, or collaborative discussions. Creating a sense of belonging can enhance trust and support.

Peer Support: Facilitate opportunities for individuals to support one another through peer mentorship, sharing resources, and providing emotional support. Peer support can create a safe space for individuals to share their challenges and seek guidance.

Collective Action: Encourage individuals to engage in collective action to address systemic issues and promote social change. This can involve identifying common goals and working together to create meaningful impact both within and beyond the supportive space.

In summary, creating supportive spaces involves establishing safe and inclusive environments, encouraging open dialogue and the sharing of diverse perspectives, and fostering a sense of community and mutual support. By incorporating these elements, individuals can feel empowered to explore their personal journeys of transformation and liberation, while also fostering understanding, empathy, and growth

within the community.

Advocate for Justice & Liberation

Stand up against injustice and advocate for the rights and well-being of marginalized communities. Address systemic oppressions and work towards dismantling structures that perpetuate inequality. Use your voice and actions to promote justice, equality, and freedom for all. Advocating for justice and liberation requires a multifaceted approach that goes beyond simply recognizing and condemning injustice. It involves actively engaging in efforts to address the root causes of systemic oppressions and working towards dismantling structures that perpetuate inequality. To truly make a difference, it is essential to deepen our understanding of the various forms of oppression and the ways in which they intersect.

One crucial aspect of advocating for justice and liberation is standing up against injustice. This means using your voice and actions to raise awareness about issues affecting marginalized communities. It involves speaking out against discriminatory practices, policies, and systems that marginalize certain groups based on factors such as race, gender, sexuality, religion, or socioeconomic status. By bringing attention to these issues, you contribute to shifting public consciousness and generating momentum for change. Addressing systemic oppressions requires a comprehensive analysis of the structures and institutions that contribute to inequality. It involves recognizing how power imbalances and privilege operate within society, and actively working to challenge and dismantle them. This may involve advocating for policy changes, supporting grassroots movements, or engaging in community organizing efforts. It is important to not only address the symptoms of injustice but also to critically examine and challenge the underlying structures that sustain it.

To promote justice, equality, and freedom for all, it is crucial to center the voices and experiences of marginalized communities. This involves actively listening and learning from those who are directly affected by systemic oppressions. By amplifying their perspectives and stories, you can help to challenge dominant narratives and promote a more inclusive understanding of justice. Advocacy for justice and liberation also requires a commitment to continuous Self-education and personal growth. It is essential to continually educate yourself about the historical and social context of oppression, as well as the ways in which it manifests in different spheres of life. This ongoing learning process allows you to develop a deeper understanding of the complex and interconnected nature of systemic injustices. Furthermore, engaging in allyship and solidarity with marginalized communities is crucial for effective advocacy. This means recognizing your own privilege, leveraging it to support marginalized voices, and actively working to dismantle the systems that grant you unearned advantages. True liberation requires collective action, and standing in solidarity with marginalized communities can help foster a sense of unity and create meaningful change.

In conclusion, advocating for justice and liberation goes beyond surface-level awareness and condemnation of injustice. It requires actively challenging systemic oppressions, addressing their root causes, amplifying marginalized voices, and working towards dismantling structures that perpetuate inequality. By engaging in ongoing education, allyship, and solidarity, you can contribute to a more just and equitable society where the rights and well-being of all individuals are valued and protected.

Integrate Spirituality & Action

Connect your spiritual beliefs and practices with meaningful action in the world. Ground your spirituality in acts of service, social justice, and the pursuit of a more equitable and compassionate society. Strive to bridge the gap between personal growth and societal transformation. Integrating spirituality and action involves going beyond the realm of personal contemplation and introspection and actively engaging with the world around us. It requires connecting our spiritual beliefs, practices, and values with meaningful action that contributes to the betterment of society. By grounding our spirituality in acts of service, social justice, and the pursuit of a more equitable and compassionate society, we can bridge the gap between personal growth and societal transformation.

Spirituality is often associated with the inner journey of Self-discovery, connecting with higher powers or universal truths, and finding meaning and purpose in life. While these aspects are important, they can become disconnected from the practical realities of the world if not integrated with action. Integrating spirituality and action involves translating our spiritual insights and values into tangible actions that address the needs of others and work towards positive change. Acts of service are essential in this integration. Engaging in acts of service means actively helping and supporting others, whether it is through volunteering, charitable work, or simply offering a helping hand to those in need. Service helps us cultivate empathy, compassion, and a sense of interconnectedness with all beings. It allows us to embody our spiritual principles by extending kindness and care beyond ourselves.

Additionally, integrating spirituality and action entails engaging in social justice work. This means addressing systemic inequalities and working towards creating a more just and fair society. It involves advocating for the rights of marginalized communities, challenging oppressive systems, and promoting inclusivity. By aligning our spiritual values with social justice, we acknowledge that spirituality goes beyond personal well-being and includes a responsibility to address the larger structural issues that perpetuate suffering and injustice. Moreover, the integration of spirituality and action requires striving for a more equitable and compassionate society. This means actively working towards creating conditions where everyone has equal opportunities and access to resources, and where compassion and empathy are valued and practiced. It involves recognizing our interconnectedness and cultivating a sense of unity that transcends boundaries of race, religion, nationality, and other social divisions.

By bridging the gap between personal growth and societal transformation, we bring our spiritual beliefs and practices into the world in a tangible and meaningful way. We recognize that personal growth and spiritual development are not separate from the well-being and progress of society. Instead, they are intimately connected, and one can enhance and inform the other. Integrating spirituality and action is a transformative process that requires Self-reflection, intentionality, and continuous learning. It encourages us to examine our own biases, privilege, and contributions to systemic issues. It challenges us to embody our spiritual values in our daily lives and engage in practices that promote justice, equality, and compassion. Ultimately, by integrating spirituality and action, we contribute to a more harmonious and just world, where our personal growth and spiritual insights are utilized for the benefit of all. It is through this integration that we can create a profound and lasting impact on ourselves, others, and society as a whole.

Embrace the Unknown

Embodying the Path-Maker archetype involves embracing the unknown and being comfortable with ambiguity. Be open to exploring new territories, taking unconventional paths, and embracing uncertainty as an opportunity for growth and discovery. Embracing the unknown is a mindset that encourages individuals to venture into uncharted territories, step outside their comfort zones, and engage with uncertainty in a proactive and positive manner. It is about being open to new experiences, ideas, and perspectives, and approaching them with curiosity and a sense of adventure. By embodying the Path-Maker archetype, individuals actively seek out opportunities to explore unconventional paths and navigate through ambiguous situations. When one embraces the unknown, they acknowledge that the future is not predetermined and that there are countless possibilities and potential outcomes. Rather than being hindered by fear or uncertainty, they view ambiguity as a fertile ground for personal growth and discovery. This mindset allows individuals to tap into their creativity, resourcefulness, and resilience, enabling them to adapt to changing circumstances and seize opportunities that may arise.

Embracing the unknown also involves letting go of rigid expectations and preconceived notions of how things should be. It requires individuals to be flexible and open-minded, ready to challenge conventional wisdom and explore alternative approaches. By doing so, they can uncover hidden opportunities and potential solutions that may not have been apparent within the confines of familiar territory. However, embracing the unknown does not mean blindly plunging into every uncertainty without careful consideration. It is a balance between taking calculated risks and being aware of the potential consequences. Path-Makers engage in thorough research, analysis, and reflection to make informed decisions, but they are not deterred by the absence of clear answers or guarantees.

In essence, embodying the Path-Maker archetype is about cultivating a mindset of resilience, adaptability, and curiosity. It involves developing the confidence to navigate uncharted waters, recognizing that growth and innovation often stem from embracing uncertainty. By being comfortable with ambiguity, individuals can pave their own unique paths, create new opportunities, and make a lasting impact in their personal and professional lives. Ultimately, embracing the unknown is a transformative journey that requires continuous learning, introspection, and a willingness to take risks. It is a mindset that allows individuals to break free from the constraints of the known and venture into the realm of possibility. By embracing uncertainty as an opportunity for growth and discovery, individuals can unlock their full potential and shape their own destinies.

Remember that embodying the Path-Maker archetype is an ongoing journey of Self-reflection, growth, and service. Be open to learning from your own experiences and the wisdom of others. Embody authenticity, resilience, and compassion as you navigate your own path and support others in their transformative journeys. By embracing the Path-Maker archetype, you can contribute to personal and collective liberation and inspire others to find their own paths towards Self-discovery, community and spiritual growth.

Chapter 3

Challenges of Walking Off-Path

A Path-Maker archetype represents individuals who are pioneers, innovators, and trailblazers. They are known for forging new and uncharted paths, whether in their personal lives or in society at large. While this archetype can be inspiring and lead to significant progress, it also comes with its share of challenges and suffering:

1. **Resistance & opposition**: Path-Makers often encounter resistance from those who are resistant to change or who are invested in the status quo. Breaking new ground can challenge established norms and traditions, leading to pushback and opposition.

2. **Uncertainty & Risk**: Creating a new path is inherently uncertain and comes with risk. There's no guarantee of success, and Path-Makers may face setbacks and failures along the way.

3. **Isolation**: Path-Makers can sometimes feel isolated or alone in their pursuits. Few people may understand or share their vision, making them feel disconnected from others.

4. **Loneliness**: The journey of a Path-Maker can be lonely because they may not have many peers or mentors who have walked a similar path. This can lead to feelings of isolation and loneliness.

5. **Fear of the Unknown**: The unknown is often intimidating, and Path-Makers must grapple with their own fears and anxieties about what lies ahead.

6. **Lack of Guidance**: Since they are creating new paths, Path-Makers may not have established guidelines or mentors to provide them with guidance and support. They must rely on their creativity and intuition to navigate uncharted territory.

7. **Resource Constraints**: Path-making often requires resources, whether financial, material, or human capital. Securing these resources can be a challenge, especially if the Path-Maker is working against established norms or institutions.

8. **Criticism & Doubt**: Path-Makers may face criticism and doubt from skeptics who question the feasibility or value of their chosen path.

9. **Burnout**: The relentless pursuit of a new path can lead to burnout as Path-Makers may feel the pressure to constantly innovate and overcome obstacles.

10. **Balancing Personal & Societal Expectations**: Path-Maker's often need to find a balance between their personal desires and societal needs. They may face the chal-

lenge of aligning their pioneering efforts with the greater good.

11. **Emotional Toll**: The stress, uncertainty, and challenges faced by Path-Makers can take an emotional toll, leading to anxiety, self-doubt, and even depression.

12. **Legacy & Impact**: There may be a constant pressure on Path-Makers to leave a lasting legacy or make a significant impact. This can be emotionally taxing and may lead to a fear of not measuring up to their own or others' expectations.

Despite these challenges, Path-Makers are often driven by a sense of purpose and a desire to make a positive difference in the world. They are resilient individuals who push boundaries, inspire change, and create new possibilities, even in the face of adversity.

Abandonment

A Path-Maker archetype represents an individual who is a trailblazer, a pioneer, and someone who forges new paths and leads the way for others. As with any archetype, there are challenges and obstacles that someone embodying this archetype may face. Abandonment challenges are one category of such challenges, and they can manifest in various ways. Here are some abandonment challenges a Path-Maker may encounter:

Isolation: Path-Makers often venture into uncharted territory, which can be a lonely journey. They may feel isolated because few people understand or support their vision. This isolation can lead to feelings of abandonment by those who don't share their enthusiasm or fail to grasp their purpose.

Lack of Support: Others may hesitate to join or assist a Path-Maker in their endeavors because they fear the risks or uncertainties associated with the new path. This lack of support can make the Path-Maker feel abandoned by their peers and colleagues.

Unpredictable Outcomes: Creating a new path involves inherent risks and uncertainties. The Path-Maker may fear that their efforts will not yield the desired results, leading to a sense of abandonment by their own dreams and ambitions.

Sacrifice: Path-Makers often make personal sacrifices in pursuit of their goals, which can include neglecting personal relationships or postponing personal desires. This can result in feelings of abandonment by loved ones or the self.

Resistance & Opposition: Breaking new ground can face resistance from various quarters, whether it's from established institutions, competitors, or even friends and family who may not understand or support the Path-Makers vision. This resistance can create a sense of abandonment, as the Path-Maker may feel like they are battling the world alone.

Self-Doubt: The challenges and uncertainties of forging a new path can lead to Self-doubt. The Path-Maker may question their own abilities and decisions, which can make them feel abandoned by their own confidence and Self-assuredness.

Burnout: The relentless pursuit of innovation and pioneering efforts can lead to physical, spiritual and emotional burnout. As a result, the Path-Maker may feel abandoned by their own energy and motivation.

It's important to note that these challenges are not exclusive to Path-Makers and may be encountered by anyone trying to break new ground or pursue a unique vision. Overcoming these abandonment challenges often requires resilience, a strong sense of purpose, empowering/rejuvenating rituals and a support system that understands and believes in the unfollowable path.

<u>Insecurities</u>

A Path-Maker archetype represents individuals who aspire to lead, innovate, and create new opportunities or ways of doing things. Like anyone else, Path-Makers can face personal insecurities and Self-doubt, but they must learn to manage these insecurities effectively to fulfill their roles. Here are some strategies for Path-Makers to deal with their own insecurities:

Self-Awareness: Recognize and acknowledge your insecurities. Self-awareness is the first step towards addressing them. Understand what triggers your insecurities and when they tend to arise.

Embrace Vulnerability: Understand that vulnerability is not a weakness but a strength. Being vulnerable and open about your insecurities can help build trust and connections with others. It also shows authenticity, which people often appreciate in leaders and Path-Makers.

Seek Support & Mentorship: Surround yourself with a supportive network of friends, mentors, and advisors who can provide guidance and reassurance when you doubt your Self. Experienced mentors can share their own experiences with insecurities and help you navigate through them.

Set Realistic Goals: Break down your aspirations and ambitions into manageable, realistic goals. Achieving smaller milestones can boost your confidence and help you see progress.

Continuous Learning: Invest in personal and professional development. Acquiring new skills and knowledge can boost your confidence and competence in your chosen path.

Mindfulness & Meditation: Practices like mindfulness and meditation can help you stay grounded and focused. They can also reduce anxiety and Self-doubt.

Accept Failure as a Learning Opportunity: Understand that setbacks and failures are part of the journey. Embrace them as learning experiences that can lead to personal growth and innovation.

Focus on Your Purpose: Remember why you chose to be a Path-Maker in the first place. Reconnect with your passion and vision to help you stay motivated and determined.

Take Care of Your Physical & Mental Health: A healthy lifestyle, including regular exercise, a balanced diet, and sufficient sleep, can have a positive impact on your overall well-being and confidence.

Practice Resilience: Develop the ability to bounce back from adversity and setbacks. Resilience is a crucial skill for Path-Makers who often face challenges and obstacles.

Celebrate Your Successes: Acknowledge and celebrate your achievements, no matter how small they may seem. This can boost your confidence and provide a sense of accomplishment.

Insecurities are a common part of the human experience, and even Path-Makers face them. The key is to develop effective strategies to manage and overcome them so that you can continue on your journey to create new paths and opportunities.

Loving Self

Embodying the Path-Maker archetype often involves forging new and uncharted routes, taking risks, and facing numerous challenges. Loving oneself is crucial for anyone in this role, as it provides the strength and resilience needed to navigate these challenges. Here are some ways a Path-Maker can love themselves:

Self-Acceptance: Accept yourself as you are, with all your strengths and weaknesses. Embrace your uniqueness and understand that imperfections are a part of being human.

Self-Compassion: Be kind and understanding toward yourself, just as you would be to a friend facing challenges.

Practice Self-compassion by acknowledging your struggles without Self-criticism.

Self-Care: Prioritize Self-care to maintain physical, spiritual, emotional, and mental well-being. This includes getting enough rest, eating healthy, exercising, and engaging in activities that bring joy.

Set Boundaries: Establish clear boundaries to protect your physical and emotional energy. Say no when necessary and protect your time and resources.

Seek Support: Don't hesitate to ask for help or seek support from friends, family, or mentors when needed. It's a sign of strength to recognize when you can't do it all alone.

Practice Mindfulness: Mindfulness meditation and self-reflection can help you stay grounded and centered during challenging times.

Positive Self-Talk: Challenge negative Self-talk and replace it with positive and affirming thoughts. Encourage yourself and remind yourself of your achievements and strengths.

Embrace Failure: Understand that failures are part of the path-making journey. Instead of seeing them as setbacks, view them as opportunities for growth and learning.

Celebrate Success: Recognize and celebrate your achievements, no matter how small. Acknowledging your progress can boost Self-esteem and motivation.

Stay True to Your Values: Living in alignment with your values and principles can provide a sense of purpose and authenticity, which can enhance self-love.

Practice Gratitude: Regularly express gratitude for the people, experiences, and opportunities in your life. This can help foster a positive outlook.

Learn from Experience: Reflect on your experiences and use them as tools for personal growth and Self-improvement.

Self-Reflection: Take time for introspection to understand your desires, goals, and motivations. This can help you make choices that align with your authentic Self.

Forgiveness: Forgive your Self for past mistakes and let go of guilt and regret. Holding onto negative emotions can hinder Self-love.

Self-Development: Invest in your personal growth and learning. Continuously acquiring new skills and knowledge can boost Self-confidence.

Remember that Self-love is an ongoing process, and it may take time to develop a deep and unwavering love for oneself, especially as a Path-Maker who faces unique challenges. Regularly practicing these principles can help you build a strong foundation of self-love, which, in turn, will empower you to overcome obstacles and make a lasting impact on the paths you choose to create.

Chapter 4

Beyond The Four Walls of Colonized Religion

A Path-Maker symbolizes someone who creates, innovates and or pioneers' new ways forward. The polar to this is something that obstructs progress, follows established routes rigidly, or resists change.

While journeying beyond the four walls of colonized religion, the Path-Maker emerges as a symbol of innovation, creativity, and pioneering spirit. This archetype embodies the essence of forging new ways forward, breaking free from the constraints of conventionality, and venturing into uncharted territories. However, inherent in the journey of progress lies the polarity of stagnation, rigidity, and resistance to change. Through the lens of Theopoetics, a methodology that integrates theology and poetics, we can explore the dynamic interplay between these polarities and illuminate the paths towards transformative growth and evolution. At the heart of the human experience lies an innate drive for exploration and discovery. The Path-Maker epitomizes this intrinsic impulse, embarking on journeys of both outer and inner landscapes. Whether in the realm of science, art, philosophy, or spirituality, the Path-Maker dares to challenge the status quo, envisioning possibilities beyond the confines of existing paradigms. With a spirit of curiosity and courage, they navigate through uncertainty, embracing ambiguity as a fertile ground for innovation. Through their creative endeavors and pioneering endeavors, they illuminate new pathways that inspire others to critically think for their Self, catalyzing collective evolution and progress.

The Polar

Yet, amidst the quest for progress, the polar force of resistance looms large. **Rooted in fear, inertia, and attachment to the familiar, this force manifests as a formidable barrier to change. It clings to established routes with a sense of security, viewing deviation as a threat to stability and order.** Whether driven by vested interests, ideological dogma, or a reluctance to confront the unknown, the polar stance obstructs the flow of transformation, perpetuating cycles of stagnation and regression. It is the antithesis to the Path-Maker's pioneering spirit, entrenched in the comfort of sameness and the illusion of control. The polar force of resistance presents itself as a formidable adversary on the journey of progress, its roots sinking deep into the soil of human psychology and societal structures. At its core lies fear, that primal instinct which triggers a cascade of reactions aimed at self-preservation. Fear of the unknown, fear of failure, and fear of losing the comforts of familiarity weave a web of apprehension, entangling individuals and institutions alike. This fear, fueled by uncertainty, becomes the breeding ground for inertia, the tendency to remain inert and motionless in the face of change. Inertia, coupled with attachment to the familiar, forms a potent cocktail that seduces individuals and societies into complacency. The allure of stability and order, embodied by the established routes and structures of the status quo, exerts a gravitational pull, compelling adherence to the known paths. Deviation from these well-trodden trails is viewed with suspicion, perceived as a threat to the fragile equilibrium carefully maintained by the forces of resistance. Thus, the polar stance becomes entrenched in the comfort of sameness, a sanctuary where the illusion of control reigns supreme.

This illusion of control serves as a shield against the inherent vulnerability of embracing the unknown. Driven by a desire to maintain power and authority, the polar stance erects barriers, both tangible and intangible, to shield itself from the winds of change. Vested interests, whether economic, political, or social, weave a tangled web of influence, entangling individuals and institutions in a web of self-serving agendas. Ideological dogma, rigid and inflexible, becomes a fortress guarding against the encroachment of divergent perspectives and alternative narratives. And beneath it all lies a reluctance—a profound aversion to confront the unknown, to step into the darkness and embrace the uncertainty that lies beyond the confines of the familiar. In its refusal to embrace the spirit of exploration and innovation embodied by the Path-Maker, the polar stance becomes a hindrance to progress, a weight that drags down the aspirations of humanity. By obstructing the flow of transformation, it perpetuates cycles of stagnation and regression, trapping individuals and societies in a relentless dance of repetition and decay. Like a ship anchored to the seabed, it prevents the voyage of discovery from setting sail, condemning humanity to drift aimlessly amidst the currents of time.

In essence, **the polar stance embodies the antithesis to the Path-Maker's pioneering Spirit.** Where the Path-Maker sees opportunity, the polar stance sees threat. Where the Path-Maker embraces change, the polar stance clings to the familiar. And where the Path-Maker seeks to chart new courses and explore uncharted territories, the polar stance remains mired in the comfort of the known, shackled by the chains of its own making. Thus, the struggle between these polarities becomes not merely a clash of ideologies, but a battle for the soul of humanity—a quest to break free from the shackles of fear and inertia and embrace the boundless possibilities that lie beyond the horizon.

Knowing Your Polar

Understanding the polar opposite to a Path-Maker is critical for anyone aspiring to embody the role of a Path-Maker for several reasons:

Awareness of Obstacles: Knowing the polar opposite illuminates the obstacles and challenges that one is likely to encounter on the path of innovation and progress. By recognizing these barriers, individuals can prepare themselves mentally and emotionally to navigate through resistance and adversity.

Strategic Planning: Understanding the polar opposite allows for strategic planning and decision-making. It enables individuals to anticipate potential roadblocks and devise strategies to overcome them effectively. By being proactive rather than reactive, aspiring Path-Makers can chart a clearer course towards their goals.

Building Resilience: Awareness of the polar opposite fosters resilience in the face of opposition. It reminds individuals that resistance and setbacks are inevitable aspects of the journey towards progress. By embracing challenges as opportunities for growth, aspiring Path-Makers can develop the resilience needed to persevere through adversity.

Fostering Empathy: Understanding the polar opposite cultivates empathy towards differing perspectives and worldviews. It encourages individuals to empathize with those who resist change, recognizing the fears and insecurities that underlie their resistance. By fostering empathy, aspiring Path-Makers can engage in constructive dialogue and bridge the gap between opposing forces.

Cultivating Innovation: Knowledge of the polar opposite stimulates creative thinking and innovation. It prompts individuals to question established norms and explore alternative approaches to problem-solving. By challenging the status quo and embracing divergent viewpoints, aspiring Path-Makers can catalyze new ideas and transformative change.

Facilitating Collaboration: Recognizing the polar opposite facilitates collaboration and coalition-building. It encourages individuals to seek alliances with like-minded individuals and organizations who share a common vision for progress. By uniting forces and leveraging collective strengths, aspiring Path-Makers can amplify their impact and effect meaningful change on a larger scale.

In essence, understanding what is polar to a Path-Maker is essential for navigating the complexities of the journey towards progress. It equips individuals with the insights, skills, and resilience needed to overcome obstacles, foster empathy, cultivate innovation, and collaborate effectively towards the realization of their vision for a better future.

A Path-Maker is Not a Pastor

In the vastness of meta-spirituality and personal growth, the traditional role of a Pastor within the confines of a colonized Church often stands in stark contrast to the unconventional figure of a Path-Maker navigating life beyond "The Four Walls of Colonized Religion." **While both figures may be associated with guiding individuals on their**

spiritual journey, the approaches, objectives, and perspectives they bring to their roles differ significantly. This chapter dives into the deep cross-analysis between a Pastor and a Path-Maker, exploring how a Path-Maker transcends the boundaries of colonized religion to offer a unique and personal guidance for those seeking a more profound connection with life and spirituality. In this exploration, we uncover the layers of dogma that can accumulate within "The Four Walls of Colonized Religion," often limiting the spiritual growth and personal evolution of their followers. **The Pastor, bound by the colonized doctrines and rituals of colonized religion, serves as a colonized shepherd within the established colonized framework, providing solace and guidance to those who are looking for comfort and sanctuary within its colonized structure: an Old Smelly Box.**

On the other hand, the Path-Maker is a *Living Symbol of transcendence,* navigating the uncharted territories beyond "The Four Walls of Colonized Religion." Freed from the constraints of colonized imperialistic beliefs, the Path-Maker embraces a more holistic and inclusive approach; meta-spirituality (multi-faith), recognizes the diversity of spiritual experiences that exist beyond "The Four Walls of Colonized Religion." Their guidance is tailored to the individual's unique journey, acknowledging that the path to enlightenment is as varied as the myriad ways people perceive and connect with the Divine. This chapter dives into the contrasting methodologies employed by these two public figures. While the Pastor may draw from Sacred texts and established colonized doctrines to illuminate the path for their congregation, the Path-Maker weaves together a tapestry of wisdom from various traditions, esoteric teachings, and personal insights. This eclectic approach allows for a more flexible and adaptive form of spiritual guidance, accommodating the ever-evolving nature of personal growth and understanding.

Furthermore, the chapter explores the evolving role of spirituality in contemporary society. As individuals increasingly seek a more personalized and authentic connection with the Divine, the rigid structures of organized religion may seem confining. The Path-Maker, in this context, emerges as a guide who not only facilitates spiritual exploration but also encourages a profound examination of one's beliefs, values, and purpose. In navigating the realms beyond "The Four Walls of Colonized Religion," the Path-Maker serves as a catalyst for the emancipation of the spiritual Self. Through an in-depth analysis of their methods, this chapter aims to unravel the intricacies of transcending established boundaries, fostering a deeper understanding of the diverse path's individuals may take in their quest for spiritual fulfillment outside "The Four Walls of Colonized Religion."

The Pastor Within the Church

A Pastor within the Church typically operates within a structured, organized, and most times a colonized religious framework. The Church serves as a spiritual hub, providing a set doctrine, rituals, and a defined community. Pastors are often seen as spiritual leaders responsible for guiding their congregation within the established doctrines of their faith. Their role involves interpreting religious texts, delivering sermons, and providing pastoral care to the members of their community. While Pastors play a vital role in fostering a sense of community and offering spiritual guidance, their focus is often confined to the colonized doctrines and traditions of the specific religion they represent (Colonized Christianity). This can limit the scope of their guidance, as it is bound by the parameters set by colonized religion, leaving little room for exploration of Self in relationship with God beyond established beliefs.

Within this structured religious framework, the Pastor's responsibilities extend beyond the pulpit and into the day-to-day lives of their congregation. They are often involved in administering sacraments, conducting religious ceremonies, and providing counseling to individuals facing personal challenges. In doing so, they act as intermediaries between the Divine and the community, interpreting religious principles to address the practical needs and concerns of their members. However, the confined nature of their role within a colonized religious setting can sometimes lead to a potential disconnect (religious trauma) between the spiritual needs of individuals and the colonized doctrinal boundaries set by the institution. The emphasis on conformity to established beliefs may inadvertently stifle personal spiritual exploration and the diverse ways individuals seek to connect with the Divine.

It is crucial to acknowledge that Pastors, like all individuals, may grapple with their own spiritual journeys and questions. The challenge lies in navigating these personal quests within the constraints of a colonized religious system that may not readily accommodate a broader spectrum of beliefs and practices (multi-faith/meta-spirituality). As society evolves and individuals seek a more personalized and inclusive approach to spirituality, there is a growing awareness of the need for Pastors to engage in conversations that transcend traditional/colonized boundaries. Encouraging open dialogue, embracing diverse perspectives, and fostering an environment that allows for the exploration of one's unique relationship with the Divine can enhance the pastoral role. In doing so, Pastors can help their congregations navigate the complexities of faith in a rapidly changing world, fostering a deeper, more individualized connection with spirituality, Self and all living things.

The Path-Maker Beyond Colonized Religion

The Path-Maker operates outside the confines of colonized religion, navigating life off-path and beyond "The Four Walls of Colonized Religions." The Path-Maker is an individual who seeks spiritual truth and personal growth beyond the boundaries set by colonized doctrines. Unlike a Pastor, the Path-Maker is not bound by institutional dogma; instead, they chart their course through the vast and unexplored territories of spirituality (meta-spirituality). A Path-Maker embraces a multi-faith approach to life, recognizing that spirituality extends beyond "The Four Walls of Colonized Religions." Their guidance is often characterized by a blend of wisdom drawn from various spiritual traditions, life experiences, dreams, philosophies, myths, and intuition. This approach allows them to offer a more inclusive and flexible form of guidance that resonates with the diverse path's individuals may travel in their spiritual journeys.

The Path-Maker's journey is a dynamic exploration, constantly evolving and adapting to the ever-changing landscapes of the soul and reality. Unencumbered by the rigidity of "The Four Walls of Colonized Religions," they traverse the terrain of meta-spirituality with an open heart and a mind free from the constraints of doctrinal boundaries. In the realm of the Path-Maker, spirituality is not confined to Sacred texts and predefined rituals; it is a living, breathing matrix held together by the cosmic threads of diverse and inclusive traditions. Their guidance is a mosaic, crafted from the collective wisdom of humanity's spiritual tapestry, enriched by personal insights and the kaleidoscope of dreams, myths, and philosophies. Unlike a traditional/colonized Pastor, **the Path-Maker is not a shepherd guarding a singular flock.** Instead, they embrace a multi-faith perspective, recognizing the inherent value in the multitude of paths that individuals may tread. This inclusive approach allows them to transcend the limitations of "The Four Walls of Colonized Religions," reaching out to those who seek a more expansive and personalized connection with the Divine. The Path-Maker's role is not to dictate but to facilitate, offering a flexible and inclusive form of guidance that resonates with the diverse spiritual journeys of those they encounter. Through this approach, they become not only navigators of the uncharted realms of spirituality but also compassionate companions, walking alongside others as they explore the depths of their own beliefs and forge a unique connection with their Self and the Sacred.

Beyond The Four Walls

The significant difference between a Pastor and a Path-Maker lies in their respective relationships with the concept of the Divine and the individual's connection to it. While a Pastor may act as an intermediary within the structured confines of a specific colonized religious tradition, a Path-Maker encourages individuals to forge a direct and personal connection with the Divine, unburdened by the constraints of colonized religion. The Path-Maker, free from the limitations of colonized institutional dogma, encourages seekers to explore their spirituality authentically. They inspire individuals to question, seek, and find their own truths rather than adhering strictly to predefined colonized doctrines. In doing so, the Path-Maker becomes a multi-faith guide for those navigating the complexities of life beyond "The Four Walls of Colonized Religions," fostering a deeper and more personal connection with the Divine.

In the ever-evolving matrix of spirituality, the contrast between a "Pastor within the Church" and a "Path-Maker navigating life beyond The Four Walls of Colonized Religions" is profound. **While the Pastor offers guidance within the colonized structured confines of a specific religious tradition, the Path-Maker encourages individuals to explore their spirituality freely and develop a stronger understanding of Self.** As seekers increasingly seek a more personal and inclusive connection with the Divine, the role of the Path-Maker becomes more relevant, offering a unique and adaptable form of guidance that transcends the boundaries of colonized religion. In this dynamic and shifting spiritual terrain, the Path-Maker emerges as a *Lighthouse, guiding individuals away from shallow waters and towards a deeper and more meaningful understanding of themselves and the interconnectedness of us all.*

In the kaleidoscope of spiritual exploration, the dichotomy between a "Pastor within the Church" and a "Path-Maker navigating life beyond The Four Walls of Colonized Religions" reflects the diverse avenues through which individuals seek connection with the Sacred. The Pastor, a custodian of established colonized traditions, serves as a beacon within the colonized confines of organized religion, offering solace and direction within the established boundaries of colonized doctrine. Conversely, the Path-Maker transcends the limitations of institutionalized/centralized beliefs, inviting seekers to embark on a personal odyssey of Self-discovery. Beyond "The Four Walls of Colonized Religions," the Path-Maker encourages a dynamic and inclusive approach to spirituality (meta-spirituality). They inspire individuals to explore the Abyss of their beliefs, fostering a deeper understanding of the inner Self and the intricate threads that weave us into the matrix of existence.

As contemporary seekers yearn for a more intimate and personalized connection with the Divine, the Path-Maker emerges as a guide on the uncharted waters of spiritual autonomy. Their role becomes increasingly relevant in navigating the evolving terrain of spirituality, offering a flexible and adaptable form of guidance that resonates with the unique journey of each individual. In this capacity, **the Path-Maker serves not as a rigid Lighthouse but as a versatile guide, helping individuals navigate away from the metaphorical death and slavery imposed by colonized dogma and towards a richer, more authentic understanding of themselves and the interconnectedness that binds all living things. In the midst of this dynamic and shifting spiritual landscape, the Path-Maker's light illuminates not only the shadows of conformity but also the diverse paths that lead to a more profound and meaningful connection with the Divine essence within and beyond the Self.**

Chapter 5

Sigma Personality

In the vast landscape of personality archetypes, the Sigma personality stands out as a unique and enigmatic force. Often associated with independence, resilience, and a trailblazing spirit, the Sigma personality is not confined by gender norms. In this chapter, we explore how a Path-Maker embodies the Sigma personality and discuss the genderless traits that define this intriguing archetype. The Sigma personality is characterized by a strong sense of independence and Self-reliance. Unlike traditional social roles, Sigma individuals do not conform to societal expectations or seek validation from others. Instead, they forge their own path, guided by internal principles and a deep understanding of their own strengths and weaknesses.

Pros:

Equality & Inclusivity: One of the primary advantages of a genderless Sigma Personality trait is the promotion of equality and inclusivity. By removing gender-specific expectations, individuals can embrace the trait without being confined by societal norms associated with masculinity or

femininity. This fosters an environment where anyone, regardless of gender, can embody the Sigma Personality and be celebrated for their unique characteristics.

Freedom from Stereotypes: Gender stereotypes often dictate how individuals should behave based on their assigned gender. A genderless Sigma Personality liberates individuals from these stereotypes, allowing them to express themselves authentically. This can lead to a more diverse and dynamic society where people are free to pursue their interests and goals without conforming to preconceived notions of what is deemed appropriate for their gender.

Empowerment & Autonomy: The Sigma Personality, with its emphasis on independence and self-reliance, can empower individuals to take control of their lives. Removing gender expectations from this trait allows everyone to embrace their autonomy, make decisions based on personal values, and navigate life in a way that aligns with their unique characteristics.

Breaking Down Gender Roles: A genderless Sigma Personality contributes to breaking down traditional gender roles. As society evolves, there is a growing recognition that certain traits are not exclusive to a particular gender. Embracing a genderless approach to the Sigma Personality challenges these stereotypes and encourages a more fluid understanding of personality traits across genders.

Cons:

Loss of Gender Identity: While a genderless approach

to the Sigma Personality promotes equality, some argue that it may lead to a loss of gender identity. For individuals who find value in expressing their gender identity through certain traits, a genderless perspective might dilute the richness of diverse gender experiences.

Resistance to Change: Society often resists change, and a genderless Sigma Personality may face backlash from those who cling to traditional gender norms. Some individuals may find it challenging to adapt to a more inclusive perspective, leading to resistance and potential social tensions.

Overgeneralization: The concept of a genderless Sigma Personality may risk overgeneralization, assuming that certain traits are universally applicable to all individuals. This oversimplification neglects the complexity of human behavior and may perpetuate stereotypes in a different form.

Cultural & Individual Variation: Different cultures and individuals have varying perspectives on gender roles and traits. Implementing a genderless Sigma Personality may not account for this diversity, potentially overlooking the nuances that shape individual experiences and preferences.

In conclusion, the Sigma personality exhibited by a Path-Maker transcends gender norms, providing a framework for individuals to express their true selves authentically. The genderless traits of independence, resilience, a trailblazing spirit, and adaptability define the Sigma personality, allowing anyone, regardless of gender, to embrace their unique journey. As society continues to evolve, recognizing and celebrating the Sigma personality as a genderless archetype encourages individuals to break free from traditional constraints and forge their own path in the pursuit of fulfillment and success.

Family Off-Path

In the expansive landscape of spiritual exploration beyond traditional paths, the role of a Path-Maker extends beyond personal discovery—it encompasses nurturing and growing a family within the ethos of Off-Path living. For those navigating this journey, whether as a parent, partner, or familial leader, the principles of compassion, authenticity, and resilience form the foundation for creating a harmonious and nurturing environment.

Embracing Authenticity in Family Dynamics

At the heart of raising a family Off-Path lies authenticity. The Path-Maker embraces authenticity not only in their personal journey but also within their familial relationships. This means fostering an environment where each family member feels empowered to explore their own spiritual path freely, without judgment or imposition. Whether through open dialogue, shared rituals, or supportive listening circles, authenticity breeds trust and unity within the family unit.

Cultivating Compassion and Understanding

Compassion is a guiding principle in navigating the complexities of Off-Path family dynamics. The Path-Maker understands that each family member may be on a unique journey of spiritual exploration, influenced by diverse perspectives and experiences. By cultivating compassion, they create a space where differences are respected, and mutual understanding flourishes. This compassion extends to supporting loved ones through their challenges and celebrating their milestones on the path to Self-discovery.

Nurturing Growth & Resilience

Off-Path living often requires resilience in the face of societal norms and expectations. As a family leader, the Path-Maker nurtures resilience by encouraging adaptive thinking and embracing life's uncertainties as opportunities for growth. This may involve fostering a spirit of curiosity and exploration, where family members are encouraged to question, learn, and evolve together. Through shared experiences and mutual support, the family grows stronger, bonded by their collective journey of discovery.

Creating Rituals & Shared Experiences

Rituals play a vital role in grounding Off-Path families in their spiritual and familial values. These rituals need not conform to traditional practices but can be creatively crafted to reflect the family's unique beliefs and aspirations. Whether through nature walks, storytelling circles, playing video games or collaborative creative projects, rituals provide opportunities for connection, reflection, and renewal. They serve as anchors in the family's journey, reinforcing shared values and fostering a sense of belonging.

Balancing Individuality and Collective Unity

A fundamental challenge for the Path-Maker is striking a balance between honoring individual spiritual paths and fostering collective unity within the family. This balance requires open communication, mutual respect, and a willingness to adapt as family members evolve in their beliefs and practices. By valuing each member's autonomy while nurturing a sense of belonging to the family unit, the Path-Maker cultivates a harmonious environment where everyone can thrive authentically. A Similar symbol would be the Mother in the context of family- the Mother cultivates, offers support and compassion; teaches patience and respect for Self as well other. A Path-Maker as a genderless archetype can be a Mother in a family dynamic.

Cultivating a Supportive Community Beyond the Family

Off-Path families often find strength and support in community connections beyond their immediate household. The Path-Maker plays a pivotal role in nurturing these connections, whether through participating in community events, joining support groups, or fostering relationships with like-minded individuals. This broader community serves as a source of inspiration, validation, and shared wisdom, enriching the family's journey and reinforcing their commitment to Off-Path living (their liberty's and freedoms).

Embracing the Journey Together

In navigating the complexities of Off-Path family life, the Path-Maker leads with courage, compassion, and a deep commitment to authenticity. By nurturing a supportive environment grounded in shared values and mutual respect, they create a sanctuary where each family member can explore, grow, and thrive on their unique spiritual journey. Through resilience, creativity, and a steadfast dedication to fostering unity, the Path-Maker shapes a family dynamic that embodies the transformative power of Off-Path living.

Final Thoughts

The archetype of the Path-Maker transcends the boundaries of conventional leadership. By daring to forge an unfollowable path, these transformative leaders challenge societal norms, inspire authenticity, and empower others to become architects of their own destinies. Their decentralized leadership style encourages a sense of community, where everyone is valued for their unique contributions. As we navigate a world yearning for change and transformation, embracing the spirit of the Path-Maker archetype can guide us towards a meta-spiritual community defined by individuality, interconnectedness, and collective growth. The archetype of the Path-Maker represents a profound departure from traditional notions of leadership. These transformative leaders are not bound by the established norms and conventions; instead, they carve out a unique and unprecedented path that others may find difficult to follow. The Path-Maker archetype embodies the spirit of innovation, audacity, and the willingness to challenge the status quo. One of the key qualities of the Path-Maker archetype is their ability to inspire authenticity in themselves and others. By fearlessly embracing their own true selves and defying colonized expectations, they encourage others to do the same. These leaders demonstrate that it is possible to be successful while staying true to one's values, passions, and individuality. They create a space where people feel empowered to express their true selves, fostering an environment of trust, acceptance, and diversity.

The Path-Makers also possess a decentralized leadership style. They recognize that every individual has unique talents, perspectives, and contributions to offer. Rather than enforcing a rigid hierarchy, they create a sense of community where each person is valued for their distinct abilities. This decentralized approach allows for a greater exchange of ideas, promotes collaboration, and encourages individuals to take ownership of their own growth and development. By embracing the Path-Maker archetype, individuals and communities can navigate a world in constant need of change and transformation. In a society longing for progress and renewal, the Path-Maker serves as a guide, helping us break free from stagnant patterns and envision new possibilities. They inspire us to question existing systems, challenge limiting beliefs, and forge our own paths towards a brighter future. Furthermore, the spirit of the Path-Maker archetype extends beyond the individual level. It promotes the development of a meta-spiritual community where people recognize their interconnectedness and work together towards collective growth. This community is characterized by a deep appreciation for diversity, cooperation, and mutual support. Individuals within this community uplift and inspire one another, recognizing that their personal growth is intimately tied to the growth of others.

In conclusion, the archetype of the Path-Maker represents a revolutionary approach to leadership and being that goes beyond conventional boundaries. By embodying authenticity, fostering community, and encouraging individuality, the Path-Makers inspire us to challenge societal norms, embrace our unique contributions, and create a meta-spiritual community driven by interconnectedness and collective growth.

In a world that yearns for change and transformation, embracing the spirit of the Path-Maker archetype can lead us towards a future defined by innovation, authenticity, and a sense of purpose.

We are Dr. Aaron C. Waldron, a dedicated Researcher, Theopoet, Dreamer, and Shaman exploring the profound intersections of religious trauma, Self-discovery, and multi-faith ministry. My journey has taken me through the complexities of spiritual exploration, the healing of deep-seated wounds, and the integration of diverse psycho-spiritual practices. Together, we are building a community that values healing, growth, and understanding.

Why We're Here
Religious trauma leaves lasting scars, affecting every aspect of life. It is a profound wound that impacts the mind, body, and spirit. My work aims to unravel these wounds, offering pathways to healing through rigorous research, community engagement, and spiritual practices that honor the rich diversity of faith traditions. This journey is not just my own—it is a shared endeavor to explore the Self, confront trauma, and embrace the spiritual diversity that shapes our world.

Your Support Matters
By becoming a patron, you are not just supporting my research; you are becoming a part of a community committed to understanding and healing religious trauma. Your contribution helps sustain this vital work, allowing me to deepen my studies, create valuable resources, and continue offering support to those on their spiritual journeys. Together, we can create a space where healing and growth are possible for everyone.

Become a Patron HERE

Transform your vision into reality with Lost Raven Studios Writing/Publishing services. Whether you're an aspiring author or an established writer, we specialize in crafting compelling e-books that captivate and inspire. From meticulous editing to seamless publishing, we ensure your manuscript shines with professional polish. Trust Lost Raven Studios to bring your words to life—because your story deserves to be told. This e-book was designed, edited, and published by Lost Raven Studios.

VISIT OUR WEBSITE HERE

Made in the USA
Columbia, SC
11 November 2024